The One In Which Bambi Tells Me To Get A Life

poems by

Jessie Ehman

Finishing Line Press
Georgetown, Kentucky

The One In Which Bambi Tells Me To Get A Life

Copyright © 2020 by Jessie Ehman
ISBN 978-1-64662-308-2 First Edition
All rights reserved under International and Pan-American Copyright Conventions. No part of this book may be reproduced in any manner whatsoever without written permission from the publisher, except in the case of brief quotations embodied in critical articles and reviews.

ACKNOWLEDGMENTS

I would like to extend my most sincere and grateful thanks to the following publications and their editors: *North American Review* for publishing "I, Lazarus" and listing it as a finalist for the 20th Annual James Hearst Poetry Prize, and *Pif Magazine* for publishing "The Bear's Feast" as well as an early version of "All My Plants Are Dead."

All the gratitude in the world goes to my mentors Jeremy Voigt and Rick Barot for their endless direction and knowledge. I would also like to thank my parents Dave and Kathy Ehman (and stepparents Charlie Dignam and Sara Harlan) for their patient support. Thank you to everyone who picks up a copy of this book and gives it a place in their hands, homes, and hearts.

Publisher: Leah Maines
Editor: Christen Kincaid
Cover Art: Zak Roth Photography
Author Photo: Zak Roth Photography
Cover Design: Elizabeth Maines McCleavy

Order online: www.finishinglinepress.com
also available on amazon.com

Author inquiries and mail orders:
Finishing Line Press
P. O. Box 1626
Georgetown, Kentucky 40324
U. S. A.

Table of Contents

Your Body As A Church After The Fire 1

Some Great Beast 2

I, Lazarus 4

Cellophane 7

At Night, My Shadow 9

The Blue Dancers 12

Sleep Paralysis 13

The Man 15

Self-Portrait With Leaves 16

Shape Shifter 18

The One In Which Bambi Tells Me To Get A Life 19

An Act Of Pure & Irrefutable Love 20

Hoard 22

The Rabbit & The Fox 24

A Sailor's Warning 26

Queen Of The Flies 28

The Bear's Feast 29

All My Plants Are Dead 30

The Second Coming, Act II 32

If This Were Salem 34

Origin Story 36

Your Body As A Church After The Fire

Let me wade through the silt of you,
the thick channels of viscous blood,
tunnels of wet earth and rot—
worms and maggots
and other sightless creatures
crawling at your peripheries.

Let me carve through the meat of you—
a taut map of sour skin and sinew,
sawing at muscle, tendon, ligament—
until I hit stone, I mean bone,
the wide shelf of rib that shelters
broken steeples and spires,
soot-stained gargoyles poised
like sentries waiting to strike,
barrel vaulted ceilings now
crumbled and collapsed,
and stained glass windows
gleaming like the eyes of wild beasts
beneath the wreckage—
the fourteen Stations of the Cross.

Let me know good can come of this,
that the world is more
than the black belch of smoke
and burning churches,
more than the way you held
my hands above my head
and asked me to beg,
or the way you folded into nothingness
like dirt at the edge of a grave.

Still make no mistake,
I am not who you think I am.
I take the glass,
a bit of the fold in Mary's skirt,
and place it like a blade
against my tongue—
see, I too, can bleed like you—
this is not an excavation,
but an exhumation.

Some Great Beast

Here in the clear black bell
of morning,

there is only silence—
lights red as poppies,

blank faces bent against the chill,
and the warm buttery glow

of bakery windows—
the sharp sweet tang

of coffee and croissants.
This is the poet's hour

caught somewhere between
real and dreaming—

a place where thoughts
drift like ghosts

along the sidewalk,
and everything is unfolding

like the wings of some great beast
awakening from slumber.

Here in this jangling cold
I could be anyone—

someone's sister or daughter
on their way to or from work,

perhaps leaving a lover's apartment
for the last time, the first time.

Perhaps walking away
from the scene of a crime

in stilettos, in kitten heels,
in sensible shoes with non-slip soles.

Perhaps this is my soul
slipping out of my mouth,

steam white and whispered
like something dirty,

disappearing into the blue black air
just like the blue black bruises

you left on my neck
and on my breasts.

If I looked up now,
would I be able to see it:

that invisible, indisputable
part of myself,

shining diamond bright
in the dawn's breath of fog—

second star to the right
and straight on 'till dreamland.

Giulio Giorello wrote that the soul
is made up of tiny robots.

If this is true—
who is it that winds the gears?

As a child you were convinced
you could speak in tongues.

Tell me: when I put my ear
to the ground, what cog

is God fixing to my spirit—
and with what teeth?

I, Lazarus

The owls are not what they seem,
        nor the deer in their moon-drunk meadows
with their noses twitching in velvet
        and their intelligent, well-deep eyes.
Perhaps they are humans wearing
        animal faces.
Perhaps we are animals wearing
        human faces.
Am I making any sense?

        I'm sorry for that night in the rain.
What I wanted to say was
        I love you,
but I suppose you already knew that.
        What I wanted to say was
*The night is only beautiful
        because it ends in morning.*

Because it ends
        the way the polished wood of a coffin sings
like a neon cross atop the highest hill in town—
        you can see yourself in its reflection,
you can see yourself
        from varnish to dirt to darkness.

Remember Jesus loves you
        even when you're buried beneath the ground.
What was that saying?
        From your lips to God's ear,
even when your lips are dry and withered away—
        a desert at dawn, at dusk—
and maggots are crawling between
        your eye sockets.
It seems impossible, I know.
        Still he died for those lips
and those maggots too.

        For whom do we die?
Sometimes the deer is more than just a deer,
        the owl more than an owl.
Weddings and funerals.

      Weddings and funerals.
The bones of your chest coming together
      to form your singular being.

The Aztecs believed that when the owl
      calls your name
your time on this earth is up.
      When you call my name I am reborn.
Oh, my dear can you ever forgive me
      for being so selfish?
I think only of myself:
      my desires, my appetites,
my insatiable thirst
      for self-destruction.

In high school I ran over a baby rabbit
      and cried for a month.
Now I watch as my useless corpse
      stumbles from the grave in daylight
just to touch the hem of your robe,
      to shed a river of tears at your feet.
Are you surprised?
      Did you really think
this would turn out differently?
      When I graze your jaw
and you sneeze—*gesundheit.*
      Bless you.
Bless your overactive olfactories.

      When you look up wearing
the face of an owl—
      your head swiveling,
a full 360 degrees
      as you open your mouth
to say my name,
      your eyes luminous,
(Cuando el tecolote canta,
      el indio muere.
When the owl sings,
      the Indian dies.)
and I crumble,

    ghost of a white-tailed deer
disappearing in mist,
    the body suddenly divided,
quartered like cuts of meat
    on the butcher's slab—
first head, then neck, then torso—
    until I am nothing but a pair
of hind legs kicking up dust.

Cellophane

My grandfather kept a closet
filled to bursting with thick, woolen coats,
their pockets a jumble of silver dollars,
bottle caps, and hard candy wrapped
in brightly colored cellophane.

He remembered every president
yet always forgot my name.
Julie, Hayley, Shelby, and sometimes
Emily or Gretchen all meant: me.

I often imagined the names of my aunts
and cousins swirling in an ambiguous haze
above my grandfather's head
until one stood out above the rest.

Sometimes, it was the name of no one at all
that he plucked from thin air,
an entire human being conjured into being—
my shadow self—
sitting where I was sitting,
talking when I was talking,
mirroring my movements
down to every involuntary tic
and synaptic impulse.

In my grandfather's living room
there were green couches with brown stripes
and on Sundays we ate bacon, eggs,
French toast, and powdered doughnuts.
We seated ourselves at the round kitchen table
beneath the painting of a man
praying over his meager supper.

After grace, my grandfather would say,
Please pass the bacon, Julie.
Would you like more eggs, Gretchen?
And I always said *yes* and *please* and *thank you.*

The night he died, my grandfather
took a hot shower, folded his towel
neatly on its rack, laid down
on the bathroom floor, and went to sleep.
It all seems deceptively easy—
doughnuts, a bit of prayer, incorrect names,
and a quiet death as if going to bed
after an exceptionally long day.

If I were to meet him again,
waiting in line for the bus
or in a crowded bookstore,

would he fold some candy into my palm—
the crinkling of the cellophane
a kind of music all its own—
saying, *Look how you've grown,
my Emily, my Julie, my Gretchen.
Look how well you've done for yourself*
as the invisible me, my other self,
rose from the depths and swallowed me whole.

At Night, My Shadow

At night,
    my shadow is unruly,
makes promises she cannot keep,

      twists herself into strange shapes,
          some familiar,
    some alien.

Now she is an alligator.

A rabbit.
A tiger.
A dog
    who unlocks his jaws
        and swallows the rabbit whole.

    Spits out the bones
like toothpicks.

You should be ashamed,
    I admonish.

We like rabbits.

Of course, she says,
baring her shadow teeth,

    we are carnivores

      after all.

My shadow
      stretches her long arms
    out to strangers
      when I'm not looking

as if to say, come here,
    let me hold you for a while

      in this particular darkness.

She sways and shimmies and invites
                    unscrupulous men in dark glasses
        home with us
              where they tie me to the kitchen chair,
light vanilla-scented candles,

      and watch my shadow dance

          across the wallpaper,

             far as the light will stretch.

When I try to call for help,
        my shadow reaches down and caresses

my throat with her fingertips,
        meaning, *Hush now,*
        don't you know what's good for you?

I miss my shadow in daylight.

        When the sun is high in the sky
and I catch glimpses of her
      around every corner
as if she is teasing me.

A little bit of ankle here,
              a flash of bare wrist there.
      Neck.
Collarbone.
          Shoulder.
     Our own private burlesque routine.

I often wonder
        if she is too much of me

and I am not enough.

      But, hush,

           there is no time for useless

musing and silly introspection.
       Or so my shadow says.

Hurry up and grab your jacket.
       Make up your face.
              The night is coming.

              We are going out.

The Blue Dancers

My mother of pearls,
mother full moon, mother tide,
mother wept at your bedside.

On some crisp fall mornings battered with frost, I fall backwards into myself, backwards into the places I carry within the folds of my pockets, the darkness there somehow familiar—a button loosed from a favorite sweater, or the outline of a cat crossing the road at dusk (its eyes aglow with light and tapetum as if they have swallowed the remaining daylight, the crook of its tail a question mark: *Who goes there and by what means*).

Was it cold when you waded to the center of the lake, weighted down with memories and the palm-warmed stones we used for skipping. (Remember watching the ripples fan out—our very own Doppler effect—to the edges of our childhood. Remember having so much power in the flick of a wrist?) Did she come to you then? Did she drag you out by your wrists and your ankles? Were you screaming, crying, your mouth a perfect O? Tell me all the ways in which she hurt you—O Mother Mayhem, O Mother Misery—O Mother of many ticking clocks all calling out the hour, all at once.

The hour, it seems, is late. Yet not as late as the night we stole out of your house to look at the stars. Were they far away, or so very close, scattered like a handful of sequins across a blue black dance hall banner, the same color as the bruises canvassing your arms, your arms themselves a canvas. I thought they were beautiful back then—your bruises, your arms—that you were beautiful, standing on the dewdrop-strewn lawn in a white sundress, the hem frayed, your feet bare and dirty. I thought of the beauty of brushstrokes—the colors both muted and bright, mottled and slightly out of focus.

I thought of stars, of dancing, of Degas and his beloved ballerinas, but you were a work of art all your own, my back against your bedroom door as we sang ourselves to sleep.

Sleep Paralysis

   I am afraid of sunlight

the way my father is afraid of caves—

    those open wounds

wet with bats and wanting.

   I call my mother.

She is decorating her closet.

    She wonders if the wallpaper

matches the throw rug—

    I tell her it does.

I tell her about a dream I had

    in which I couldn't wake up.

I was lying in bed and screaming.

    I was crawling across the carpet

with my eyes sewn shut,

    but no one could hear me,

no one could see me.

    I tell her I think I have sleep paralysis.

That's nice, she says,

    I'm thinking of wainscoting in the hallway.

Occasionally my neighbors

    will have shouting matches at 2am.

I will cower in my pajamas

    beside the steadying hum of the furnace,

wishing that I could give them

    the thing they so desperately desire.

When I turn off the lights,

    a tiny windup bird

flits about my ceiling fan.

    His beak unzippers and silver coins fall out.

He vanishes—a magic trick.

    Come morning: a flurry of wings

at the door like darkness.

    Who is it?

I let the wings in,

    let the darkness in,

let it curl up on the couch

    like a particularly well-fed housecat.

Let it raid my refrigerator

    until there are no more apples.

The Man

at night the woods climb through my window first one branch
and then another until the walls pulse wetly with twigs and roots
moss and dirt and mud there are arteries and ventricles and veins too
an entire cardiovascular system buried just beneath the surface
except I am not beneath the surface but in my bed the sheets
thrown back the exposed mattress a riot of pillows and blankets
my arms and legs suddenly bound wrist and ankle with vines thick
as pythons that come alive and writhe and hiss snap and squeeze
while somewhere above my head a violent rustling begins the trees
take up their instruments and start to play but the orchestra is wrong
all wrong the violins are wailing wall wailing or is it the trees
that dreadful screeching splintering that sounds as if the trees
are incinerating as if the trees are on fire and at some point the fire
must cause a branch to break loose and strike out on its own
to force its way inside my mouth that must be it to force its way
between my teeth and down my throat and I cannot speak
I cannot see for the darkness that fills the room like smoke
for where there's smoke there's fire and also the smell the stink
of skin of flesh and fur on fire of rabbits running crazed like rabbits
between light and shadow and I am the rabbit I am the shadow
upon the wall flickering like the eerie light of a blood moon swollen
and bloated bleeding from the mouth flickering in and out of sight
between the trees until I flicker no more and my light goes out
completely and so it goes and so it goes as the shadows retreat
into their corners and the branches withdraw their bony fingers
the vines loosen their grip and the roots slither beneath the ground
I mean the carpet I mean the ground and the man where did he come
from when did he become a man climbs out the window from which
he came at least I think never to be seen again but the fire still remains
the fire still roars and rages and rages and roars ever onward

Self-Portrait With Leaves

In the city the leaves all fall at once.
I open my door to a wall of skeletons

shifting slightly like guilty children.
I'm sorry I—

spilled milk across the pages
of your favorite novel,

fed cauliflower to the dog
waiting patiently under the table,

watched you chopping onions in secret
and now I can't stop crying,

now I—
Streetside, leaves entomb cars

like windblown sarcophagus,
cars like dismembered bodies

buried deep beneath the snow.
You can dig and dig forever

to find only remnants,
perfectly preserved remains—

a finger, a hand, a strand of hair,
or a pinkie toe; a hubcap,

a fender, the steering column—
each blackened and burnt out

by frostbite, by rust and exposure.
Instead of driving we walk to work,

carrying shovels and leaf blowers,
the occasional garbage bag.

At night, we host bonfire after bonfire
until the apartment blocks flicker,

stucco-sided jack o' lanterns
on the cusp of Halloween.

Still the leaves find their way inside
through mail slots and chimneys,

open windows and cracks in the drywall,
the small gap between door and floor—

and don't you even think
about looking under the bed.

As the piles of debris rise to the eaves,
I wonder if I, too, am made of leaves.

If I unstitched my flesh row by row,
tack by hasty tack,

would I find myself filled with the rotten,
the marbled and moldy-veined,

the long claw of winter
tapping on the windowpane.

Would I find myself bursting at the seams
with the spoiled spoils of fall—

all those dried and dusty organs
crowded inside this burlap sack—

crab tree and apple, aspen and alder,
maple and madrona, birch and yew—

this shuddering scarecrow planted
against a backdrop of plowed earth,

purple moonshine mountains,
and fallen stalks of the sweetest sweet corn.

Shape Shifter

when I kissed you
    you said
        I'm sorry it took so long
    and it's true
        I've waited years
    lifetimes
slipping into one body
after another

    body after body
        sometimes human
    sometimes not
        until I found myself here
    in this moment
leaves falling

to the ground
    like wet gods
        that one is Hercules
    that one is Zeus
        until you go back inside
    and I pick up my boulder
shed my skin
until everything
    is pink and new
        raw and whorled
    like the flesh of a fish
        split down the middle
    their names
caught in my throat

like a net
    or a prayer

I grow gills
    at your empty altar
and head upstream
    is this what we mean

when we say eternity

The One In Which Bambi Tells Me To Get A Life
After Dean Young's "Gizzard Song"

I keep losing all the spoons in my house.
What could it mean? There are never enough socks left
in the dryer and I swear someone is living inside my closet.
I dreamt last night that I wrote an essay
about my grandmother whom I have never met.
I described an old photograph in which she is wearing
some sort of brace that looks like a medieval torture device.
I don't know if such a picture exists. *Was she very small?*
someone asked. *Very small*, I said. *And very cruel.*
Now snow is falling from the trees outside my window
and there is a standoff on the highway where a man
is threatening his own life with a knife.
Can you tell me if everything will be okay?
A ceramic deer head is mounted on my kitchen wall
and he only speaks in riddles. *I weigh nothing,
but you can still see me, feel me*, he sings. *I am a hole.
A hole in your heart.* Remember all those stories
we were told as children? They are much darker in reality.
Sometimes the girl never makes it out of the woods.
Sometimes she arrives too late to save the one she loves.
Tell me, what happens after the wolf tricks Little Red
into eating her grandmother? I don't know. I don't know.

An Act Of Pure & Irrefutable Love

The night of your ten-year reunion, we lay on the floor of a classic car showroom, warm and full, talking about the Donner Party after having eaten scalloped potatoes, seasoned asparagus, dinner rolls soft with butter, and baked chicken marinated in cranberry sauce. *Makes sense,* you said. *Wouldn't anyone do the same,* you said. *I bet humans taste more like pork than chicken.*

When you were young, you watched rats eating rats outside your bedroom window and there was so much blood, enough blood to fill a pitcher at a lemonade stand, enough blood to run red in the gutters, enough blood to run all the way to the ocean with its toxic algal blooms and red tides. During communion Jesus' blood is shed for you, his body broken for you, look, everything here is for you, even if the grape juice is more purple than red, it still tastes like wine if only you try hard enough.

In the time of the rats, your mother left your pet hamster in the open garage overnight because the sound of its wheel was giving her a headache. Come morning, its frozen body was swallowed by the frozen earth. At the makeshift funeral, your eyes and nose were running, your hands and feet frozen like the hamster's lifeless corpse. Was your heart then frozen too?

Did you know that our hair and fingernails keep growing long after we've died? Did you know that the compulsion to eat one's own hair is called Rapunzel Syndrome, or trichophagia? Cats and dogs will often eat their owners after their death if they are left alone with the body, and in nature, mother bears, lions, and monkeys will eat their young if they are too weak to survive.

It was raining outside when we watched the film about a hero returning after a long journey. The townspeople were so happy to see him they devoured his body on the spot. Only his clothing remained—a velvet waistcoat and a single tufted slipper. Never before had the townspeople felt so correct, so righteous and full of truth. Afterwards they called it an act of pure and irrefutable love.

Is love nothing but a desperate act of consumption? A vain attempt to possess something that does not belong to us? Snow White took a bite of the poison apple, Goldilocks stole the porridge, Hansel and Gretel were roasted alive in an oven. Have we not been warned as many times over, even as we continue picking up light and breadcrumbs, marching ever forward into the reckless wheel of night, hoping it is not the color red, or blood, or open mouths, but love that finds us there.

A red scarf in snow—
bloody bloom against the pale
stretch of skin now quiet.

Hoard

You will never be beautiful,
my father tells me
in the same voice
he used to say,
*No one will ever love you
if you cannot
learn to love yourself.*

Yet how can I grasp
this love language,
when even the hawk falling
from the power lines—
its tail feathers ablaze,
a real life phoenix—
has its own kind
of rapture.

And the lightning.
And the thunder.
And the boy who trails behind—
his job to pick up the bodies
before they catch the brush on fire.

The boy.
The bird.
The bodies.

I roll the words over my tongue,
cool to the touch,
like the glass marbles
I collected as a child:

*Catseye
Agate
Alabaster*

*Oxblood
Tiger
Turtle*

Bumblebee

My father has saved these
amongst other keepsakes
from my childhood—
comic books,
dollhouses,
stuffed animals,
and photographs.

Maps to places that no longer exist.

As if he raised a collection
of objects and not a daughter.

As if my body is a jigsaw
broken into fault lines
and missing pieces,
waiting to be fitted together again.

Just call me humpty dumpty—
my turn-ons include eggshells
and packaging tape.

In my dreams,
I wade towards him
on a sea of broken
furniture and baseball caps.
Isn't the ocean beautiful?
my father says,
wearing the face
of someone who doesn't know
they are drowning.

I want to call out:
The ocean is me.
I am the ocean.
My beauty is everywhere.

But the next wave
pushes him under.

The Rabbit & The Fox

If I loved you—
what would become of your eyes,
fringed as they are with impossibly long lashes?
Or the way you hide your teeth when you speak,
but not when you laugh?

What would become of your hands,
which have never known the callused shell
of hard work,
which have never carried the burden of passion,
like a child swaddled in dirty rags,
from door to door looking for shelter?

There is a certain kind of forgiveness
in the softness of your body—
a special unraveling of time—
the way it curls into my own
like a question mark,
asking without words what comes next.

Is there redemption too
in the newness of your skin—
the blank page of it;
the sweet cream of it;
unblemished by sunlight
or age
or wrinkles—
how it blushes and bruises
at the slightest touch,
how the soft scrub of stubble
above your upper lip
reminds me of a desert
that has never felt the shadow of rain.

If I loved you—
what would become of the fullness of those lips?
The way you chew with your mouth open,
speak with your mouth open,
and kiss with your mouth open.
The way your words
are always coming and going,

saying their long goodbyes
like lovers on a train platform;
the way your lips strike
my own like lightning—
fast as a viper,
or the snake that tempted Eve.
Only you are Eve and I am the apple,
red and ripe in your hands,
and you are
hungry, hungry, hungry
for any kind of knowledge.

If I loved you—
what would happen when you found out
that I had not been the deer in the headlights
or the rabbit running headfirst into danger,
but the fox all along.
The nape of your neck
plush between my teeth.

A Sailor's Warning

Would it be so bad if Odysseus
never found his way home?
If he stayed with Circe on her island,
his crew of swine forever
burying their snouts in the sand,
getting fat off wild fruit and ferns.

You never know,
they might be happier as pigs
than they ever were as men.

Or if the animals in Pi's rowboat
were really just ordinary people
who killed each other like animals.
Because they were starving
and dehydrated.
Because they wanted to know
what humanity looks like
if you slice it down the middle,
gnaw off its legs at the kneecaps,
and make it beg.

Is it really so horrible?
People die every day at sea.

When I was younger,
my father set me adrift
in a fiberglass canoe.
I dropped my oar in the water
and turned in lazy circles
all afternoon.

I think my compass is broken.
It keeps pointing towards you,
but you are not here.

You are that place on the map
marred by rising tides and dizzying eddies.
You are an underwater cave.
A whirlpool.
Tendrils of seaweed reaching up

from the deep to ensnare
thrashing legs and ankles.

Who do you think you are?
Poseidon?
Neptune?
King Triton?

I long for that rippling silence
when I wake at daybreak,
reach for the notebook and write:
This morning, I didn't think of you.
Not once.

The sky is red—
what was that about a sailor's warning—
and, later, the man at the bookshop
talks about growing up in the South
and pulling himself up by his bootstraps.

In another lifetime, you and I cried tears
of laughter, backs against the kitchen floor.
There were sirens in the alley
and everything was so warm
and bright in the way that stars
are before they return to darkness.

Queen Of The Flies

There are so many flies in my apartment.
        They lay eggs in the cats' food,
which swell fat into maggots,
        which grow into more flies
and lay still more eggs.
        I chase them with a plastic fly swatter,
spilling brightly colored guts
        across walls and tabletops,
growing increasingly bloodthirsty
        for the piles of bodies
crumpled like tin soldiers,
        the limp wings
swept into napkins,
        even the sickly sweet stench
of rotting fruit.
        I think:
Angles.
        Trajectories.
Aerodynamics.
        Like a scientist observing a reaction,
I am calm.
        Calculated.
I think: American Psycho.
        I think: American Beauty.
American History X.
        And perhaps there is something
uniquely American
        in the way I appropriate death.
Give it a name and a leash.
        Let it sleep under my roof.
And call it my own.
        Please forgive me,
I mumble in my sleep.
        I am not a killer.
Still the flies slip into my mouth,
        one by one by one,
filling me with words and rumblings
        that are not my own.

The Bear's Feast

While you were away,
I listened to a podcast about bears.
Bears caught in flash floods,
bears walking upright,
bears flirting with evolution
in the wild north of Alaska.
And this one bear, in particular,
stealing peaches from a suburban
backyard in Georgia.
Each night, the bear would return
to the same yard and strip the trees bare.
In the morning, the homeowners
awoke to carnage—
*It seems more than a little indecent
how bears these days have no manners—*
peach pits strewn across the lawn
like shell casings, and the fruit itself:
skin torn from the body,
revealing the sticky, pulpy insides
sluicing to the ground
like bright organs.
The perpetrator nowhere in sight,
save for a bit of black fur
caught on a stray branch, a fence post.
A macabre sex act,
the police must have said,
shaking their heads in disbelief.
*The Jackson Pollock of bears—
The Peach: A Study In Excess.*
And there's something in here
about bears and love and loss
and peaches,
and I wish I could tell you
why it means so much to me.

All My Plants Are Dead

Forgive me Father for I have sinned.
I tried to read the classics,
to turn the pages of Melville and Dickens and Joyce,
to recite Keats and Williams and Rilke.
I tried to keep up appearances—
to floss my teeth and keep my plants alive
much like an aquarium I continue tending
long after all the fish are dead.

Yesterday I went to a bar and listened
as my friends discussed Descartes
over nachos, Blue Moon, and karaoke,
watched them vomiting light and laughter
in the alleyway out back—
their bodies loose-limbed and loved
like branches caught up in an autumn breeze,
people driving from across the country
just to glimpse that sudden burst of color.

Isn't it a laugh?
Isn't it a riot?
Those moon-drunk boys.
Those brewhouse philosophers
and brown bottle poets.
How they prance and pose and postulate.
How they preen and clean
each other's feathers.
How they—

I went home early and knitted an afghan.
I knit one, pearl two, knit one, pearl two
until my stitches flowed out the window
and into the street,
until small animals played hide and seek
between the folds,
until the neighbor's dog dragged it off the page
and out of existence,
fog filling the valley like a clear bowl
swimming with ghosts.

In the morning I crossed myself
and the roadside crosses were painted black.
Black like the velvet meadows
of your father's childhood
where he spent summer evenings fishing
for bats in the near dark of twilight.

At the behest of pocket change and the CDC,
he threaded meal worms and gnats
with nimble fingers,
casting his line toward the heavens
like a tin can on a string—
Hello, God, can you hear me now—
hoping against hope for a catch,
for that instant when hook pierced flesh
sending those little leather clad gods
plummeting to the ground
and into the waiting burlap sack.

It was a real bargain,
you remember your father telling you.
At fifty cents a bat, he could fuel
an entire summer's worth of fun.
For six bats he could get dollar cones
at the ice cream parlor downtown—
The Big Scoop—with two friends.
For twelve he could see some actress'
left breast in some film
about cowboys in space.
(What a time to be a young boy in Texas!
What a time to be alive!)

Here, in this century, I have only space
in its cyclical yet reassuring infinity,
its slow churned inevitability.
Here my hands are empty;
my head, my heart empty.
The sky outside my window is empty too,
drowning in Van Gogh post-ear blue
and echoing the afterimage of so many
small and winged things in flight.

The Second Coming, Act II

I'm sorry I might not stay awake for this.
A red curtain opens and closes, opens and closes,
as tiny players take the stage, one by one by one.

My mother appears, center stage,
and tells the story of a little girl
who is followed home by two ghosts—
a mother and a daughter.
The girl is especially afraid of the daughter
who carries a cloth doll and won't stop crying.

I look behind myself every time
I walk through a door—just to make sure
nothing has followed me into the room.
The little girl refuses to go to school
the next day, my mother says.
One pair of ghosts is enough.

In Catholic school, my best friend told me
the Second Coming had come and gone
and left us behind. To this day, I always feel
as if I am running to catch up.
Most everyone my age has children.
I have three cats and can't sleep through the night.

On weekends I am afraid to leave the house.
Instead I lie in bed and dream terrible dreams
of car crashes, my father having a stroke,
or my mother slowly dying of cancer.
In one I am running through a field of bullets
while strangers bleed out into the nearby river.

Still I sleep and sleep and somewhere
a red curtain opens and closes, opens and closes,
the players line up, take center stage—
tiny cloth dolls shaped like me, like my mother,
like the one I loved and left behind.

A shift. A spotlight changes colors.
My mother moves on, speaks of a janitor
who hung himself in the basement,

but never stopped coming to work.
Outside the day moon—far away and placid,
a hangnail waiting to rip, to tear open wide.

If This Were Salem

If this were Salem,
I would long to feel the weight
of ropes bound tight against my wrists,
the crackle of flames hot beneath my feet,
the whisper of a single word
borne honeysuckle sweet on the wind
and shivery as a phantom—
Witch.

If this were Salem, you would
have chopped the wood yourself
even if it took all afternoon.
Even if sweat rolled
down your back like thunder.
You would have lit the match
and fed the fire with your own hands—
bread given of your own body.
If there was no wood,
you would have filled my pockets
with smooth and heavy stones—
stones for bruising skin and breaking bones.
One for each day you served me
alphabet soup stewed from your own words
regurgitated there in the bowl,
the letters crawling
down my throat like spiders,
writhing in the pit of my stomach
like a snake with many heads—
or maybe just two.
But words can never hurt me.

If this were Salem, you would have read
the list of my crimes out loud.
Did you find me conversing with crows
in a pentagram-filled clearing?
Or bathing in the blood of a newborn calf
sacrificed under the full moon?
Perhaps I slept with your brother?
Or, worse yet, your sister?
In the end, the scale of my crimes
would not matter—

a thin veil for a truth
far more horrible than the last:
*I am yet another woman
who has outlived her usefulness.*

If this were Salem,
my parents would be the next in line
to light the fire,
to cast the stones,
to hold my head beneath the water.
My father would yell the loudest—
Burn the witch!
Drown the witch!
Kill the witch!
My mother adding cries of:
Slut!
and *Bitch!*
and *Whore!*
You would kiss me one last time—
a kiss with no kindness—
before you whispered,
*I hope you burn in hell
as you have burned here on earth.*
Only then would I cry out
in a language suddenly beyond my grasp
like a dream at the edge of morning:
Please.

Instead this is not Salem.
You leave me with nothing.
Neither the burning itch of flame,
nor the choking flood of water.
Not even the mercy of a loveless kiss.
Not even goodbye.
And so, hands and feet unbound,
pockets unburdened,
my sisters asleep inside their graves,
I walk free.
That is punishment enough.

Origin Story

In dreams I sit on the couch where your father courted
death at the bottom of a bottle and your mother kissed
the lips of ghosts and other women where your brother
fast forwarded through all the sex scenes and said
this is the best part of the movie but it's kind of gay
I go back further watch you fall asleep inside your toy
chest a soft footed pearl nestled deep within an oyster
watch the babysitter call the police the walls flashing
red and white and blue just like the American flag
like the Fourth of July or a frosting topped birthday cake
eaten with small and greedy hands during the summers
when my cousins and I practiced catching fireflies
in Western Ohio now we drive past buildings lit up
like firecrackers like the whole city is one big parade
at night one tent sized picnic blanket laid out special
for us you grip the steering wheel say you want to go
camping in the middle of nowhere so let's do it my love
let's go ice fishing in Alaska let's rent a cabin with a real
wood burning stove and wear flannel and deerskin
and waders up to our nipples praying to the gods
of the North the old gods who existed before war
before language and man with his sharpened tools
and bows and arrows a time when the land was alive
and even the trees had faces let me kiss you here
on this sacred holy ground caught between river
and mountain not with my lips but with my nose to yours
ice tipped from wind and chill your warmth flooding
me filling me up like a pitcher collecting moonlight
as the earth spins and spins and snow falls from the sky
like ashes like airborne leaflet propaganda hooray hooray
it all ends today until we all fall down until flowers
sprout in our pockets and thorns pierce our sides
and Jesus weeps and weeps in his modern heaven
while the deer go on drinking deep in their cups
the fish in their riverbed graves the fox in their jewel
strewn hollows and we are the king the queen of cups
of strawberry wine and starlight and the old gods say
stop look at all this darkness but we don't see it we don't
feel it we are safe so long as we don't look it in the eye